Viola Time Joggers

Piano accompaniment book

Kathy and David Blackwell

Teacher's note

These piano parts are written to accompany the tunes in *Viola Time Joggers*. They are an alternative to the viola duet accompaniments or audio tracks, and are not designed to be used with those items. A separate violin piano accompaniment book is available providing parts for when violas play together with violins using *Fiddle Time Joggers*.

Kathy and David Blackwell

OXFORD
UNIVERSITY PRESS

OXFORD
UNIVERSITY PRESS
Great Clarendon Street, Oxford OX2 6DP,
United Kingdom

Oxford University Press is a department of the University of Oxford.
It furthers the University's objective of excellence in research, scholarship,
and education by publishing worldwide. Oxford is a registered trade mark of
Oxford University Press in the UK and in certain other countries

This collection © Oxford University Press 2005, 2013, and 2022

Unless marked otherwise, all pieces (music and words) are by Kathy and David Blackwell and are
© Oxford University Press. All traditional and composed pieces are
arranged by Kathy and David Blackwell and are © Oxford University Press.
Unauthorized arrangement or photocopying of this copyright material is ILLEGAL

Kathy and David Blackwell have asserted their right under the Copyright,
Designs and Patents Act, 1988, to be identified as the Composers of this Work

Database right Oxford University Press (maker)

Impression: 1

All rights reserved. No part of this publication may be reproduced,
stored in a retrieval system, or transmitted, in any form or by any means,
without the prior permission in writing of Oxford University Press

Permission to perform the works in this anthology in public
(except in the course of divine worship) should normally be obtained from
a local performing right licensing organization, unless the owner or the occupier
of the premises being used already holds a licence from such an organization.
Likewise, permission to make and exploit a recording of these works
should be obtained from a local mechanical copyright licensing organization

Enquiries concerning reproduction outside the scope of the above
should be directed to the Music Rights Department, Oxford University Press, at
music.permissions.uk@oup.com or at the address above

ISBN 978-0-19-356226-4

Cover illustration by Martin Remphry

Music and text origination by Katie Johnston
Printed in Great Britain on acid-free paper by
Halstan & Co. Ltd, Amersham, Bucks.

Contents

1. Bow down, O Belinda (*duet*) 4
2. Under arrest! 5
3. Someone plucks, someone bows (*duet*) 6
4. Down up 6
5. Two in a boat (*duet*) 7
6. London Bridge (*duet*) 8
7. Fast lane 9
8. In flight 10
9. Lift off! 11
10. Katie's waltz 12
11. Copy cat (*duet*) 13
12. Tap dancer 14
13. Rhythm fever 15
14. Here it comes! 16
15. So there! 17
16. Rowing boat 18
17. Ally bally (*duet*) 19
18. Tiptoe, boo! 20
19. Travellin' slow 22
20. C string boogie 23
21. Off to Paris (*duet*) 24
22. Clare's song 26
23. City lights 25
24. Daydream 28
25. On the prowl 29
26. Summer sun 30
27. Phoebe in her petticoat (*duet*) 31
28. Ready, steady, go now! 32
29. Cooking in the kitchen (*duet*) 33
30. Happy go lucky 34
31. The mocking bird (*duet*) 36
32. Algy met a bear (*duet*) 37
33. Listen to the rhythm 38
34. Cattle ranch blues 40
35. In the groove 41
36. Stamping dance 42
37. Distant bells 43
38. Lazy scale 44
39. Runaway train 45
40. Rocking horse 46
41. Patrick's reel 47
42. Calypso time 48
43. Tudor tune 49
44. Chopsticks for two (*duet*) 50
45. Carrion crow (*duet*) 51
46. Flying high 54
47. Viola Time 52

1. Bow down, O Belinda

American folk tune

2. Under arrest!

KB & DB

3. Someone plucks, someone bows

Traditional
Words KB & DB

4. Down up

C string special

KB & DB

5. Two in a boat

American folk tune

6. London Bridge

English folk tune

7. Fast lane

KB & DB

Try even faster the second time through!

8. In flight

9. Lift off!

10. Katie's waltz

KB & DB

11. Copy cat

KB & DB

12. Tap dancer

KB & DB

13. Rhythm fever

KB & DB

14. Here it comes!

KB & DB

15. So there!

KB & DB

16. Rowing boat

KB & DB

17. Ally bally

Scottish folk tune

18. Tiptoe, boo!

KB & DB

13
p
sf
p
16
sf
p
sf
19
p
f
sub. p
f
23
sub. p
pp
Boo!
(shout!)
8ve
sfz

19. Travellin' slow

KB & DB

20. C string boogie

C string special

KB & DB

* Turn around or, if you are sitting, stand up and sit down again!

21. Off to Paris

French folk tune

22. *Clare's song:* next page

23. City lights

KB & DB

Nos. 22 and 23 are reversed to avoid a page turn.

22. Clare's song

KB & DB

19
mp
dim.
mp
23
27
32
rit.
p
p

24. Daydream

C string special

KB & DB

25. On the prowl

C string special

KB & DB

26. Summer sun

KB & DB

27. Phoebe in her petticoat

American folk tune

28. Ready, steady, go now!

KB & DB

29. Cooking in the kitchen

KB & DB

30. Happy go lucky (for lain)

KB & DB

19
f
f
23
28
32
ff
ff

31. The mocking bird

American folk tune

32. Algy met a bear

KB & DB
Words anon.

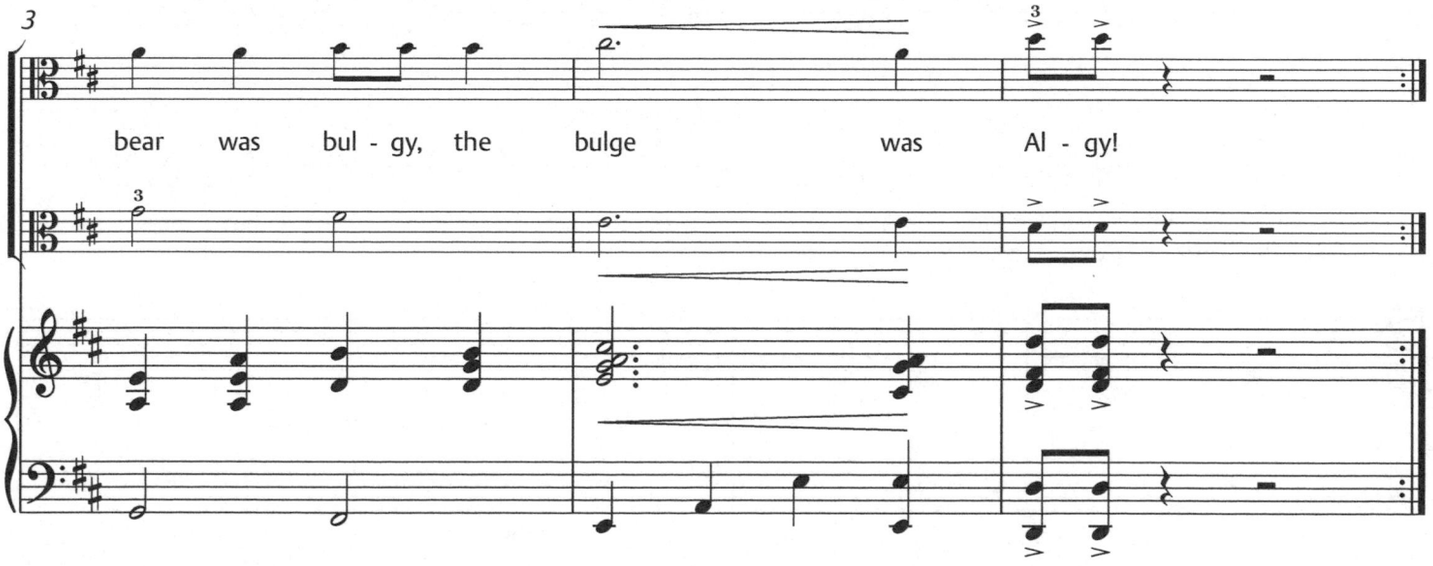

33. Listen to the rhythm

KB & DB

17
vi - o - la.
Mi - nims sound like this:
Half - notes sound like this:
21
Mi - nims sound like that!
Half - notes sound like that!
25
Lis - ten to the rhy - thm on my vi - o - la.
Se - mi - breves like
Whole-notes sound like
30
this:
this:
Se - mi - breves like that!
Whole-notes sound like that!
ff

34. Cattle ranch blues

KB & DB

35. In the groove

KB & DB

36. Stamping dance

Czech folk tune

37. Distant bells

KB & DB

38. Lazy scale

KB & DB

39. Runaway train

C string special

KB & DB

The music is written out in full in the viola part.

40. Rocking horse

41. Patrick's reel

42. Calypso time

KB & DB

43. Tudor tune

C string special

KB & DB

44. Chopsticks for two

C string special

KB & DB

45. Carrion crow

46. *Flying high:* page 54

47. Viola Time

KB & DB

Nos. 46 and 47 are reversed to avoid a page turn.

17
1.
mp
19b
2.
pizz.
Fine
mp
23
cresc.
cresc.
26
rit.
D.𝄋 al Fine
mf
mf

46. Flying high

KB & DB